Robert Adams

Hope is a risk that must be run

Hartmann books

Fondation Stichting

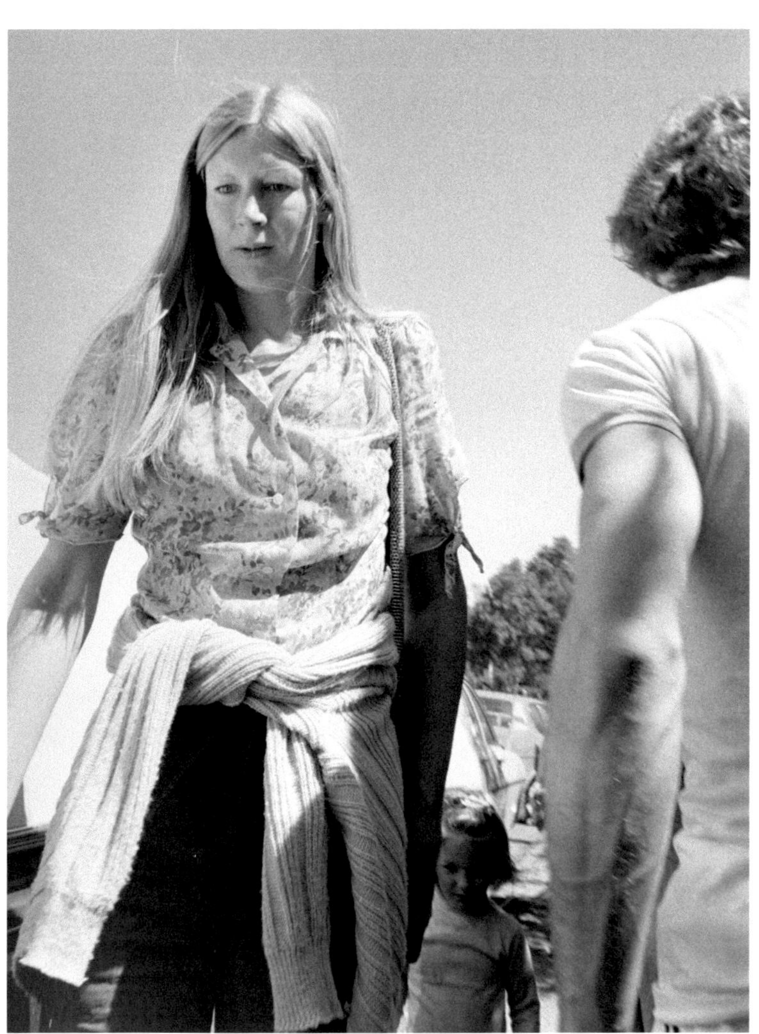

Today the matter of hope is inescapably urgent. Among the threats to our collective and individual prospects are those of terrorism and the systematic abuse of the natural world we share. What many of these jeopardies have in common is that, as a species, we inflict them upon ourselves.

These photographs were made by Robert Adams between 1979 and 1982 near a nuclear weapons plant in Colorado. Citizen protest led to the closing of the plant in 1989, but damage to the environment and public health remains.

As we again weigh the cost of possible nuclear catastrophe, what seems especially noteworthy about the pictures now are the acts—however small and fleeting—of concern, tenderness, and care for our fellow human beings.

Joshua Chuang

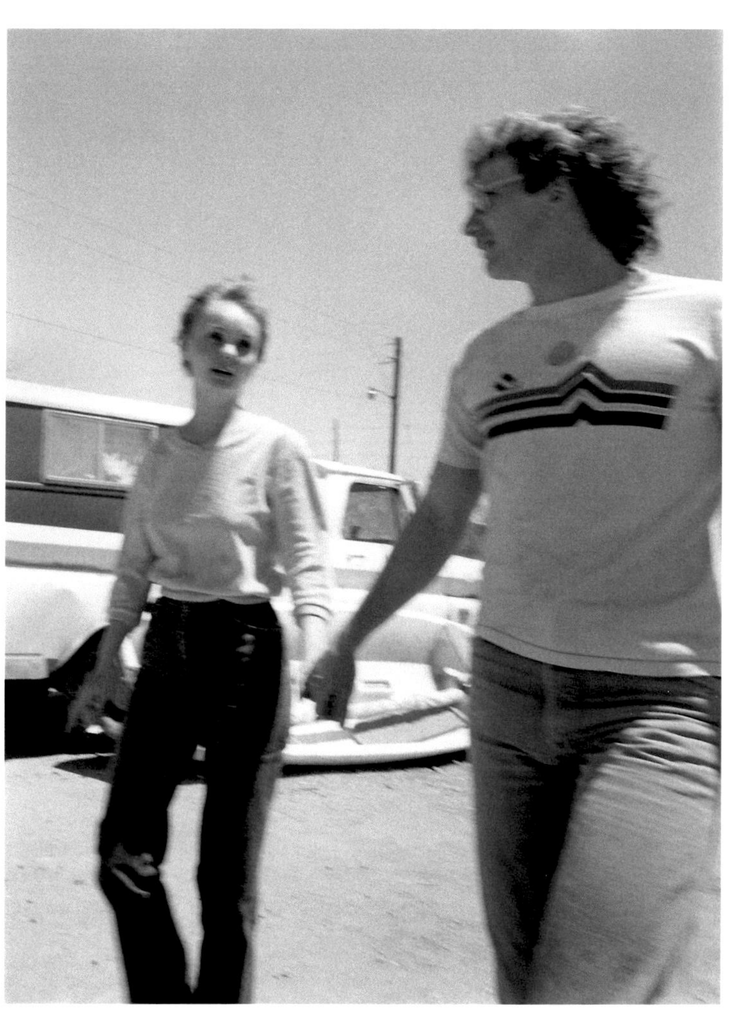

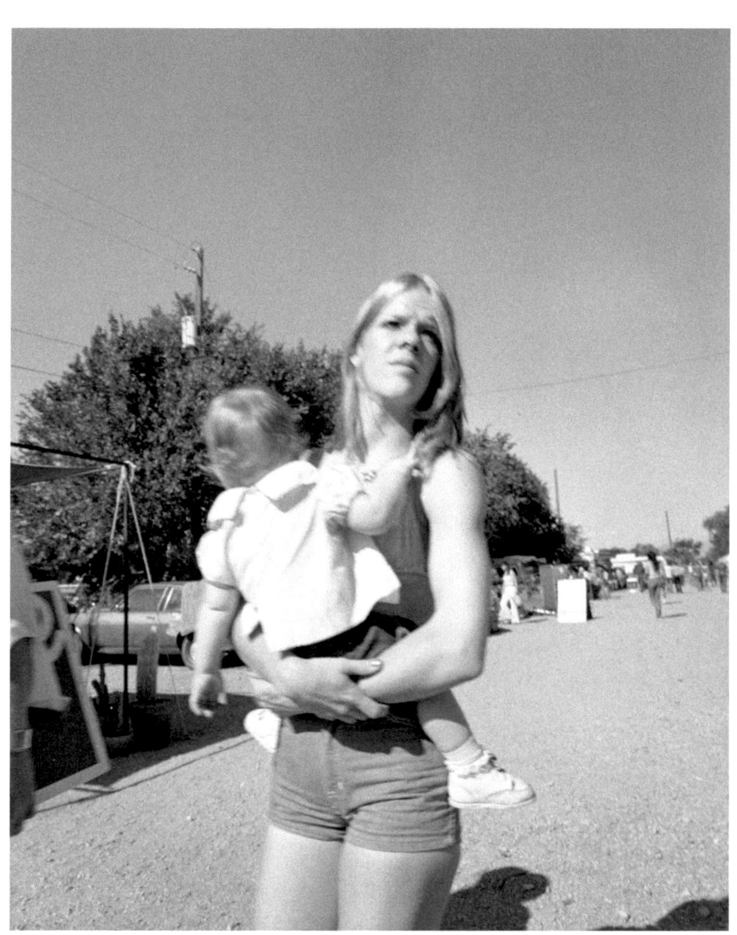

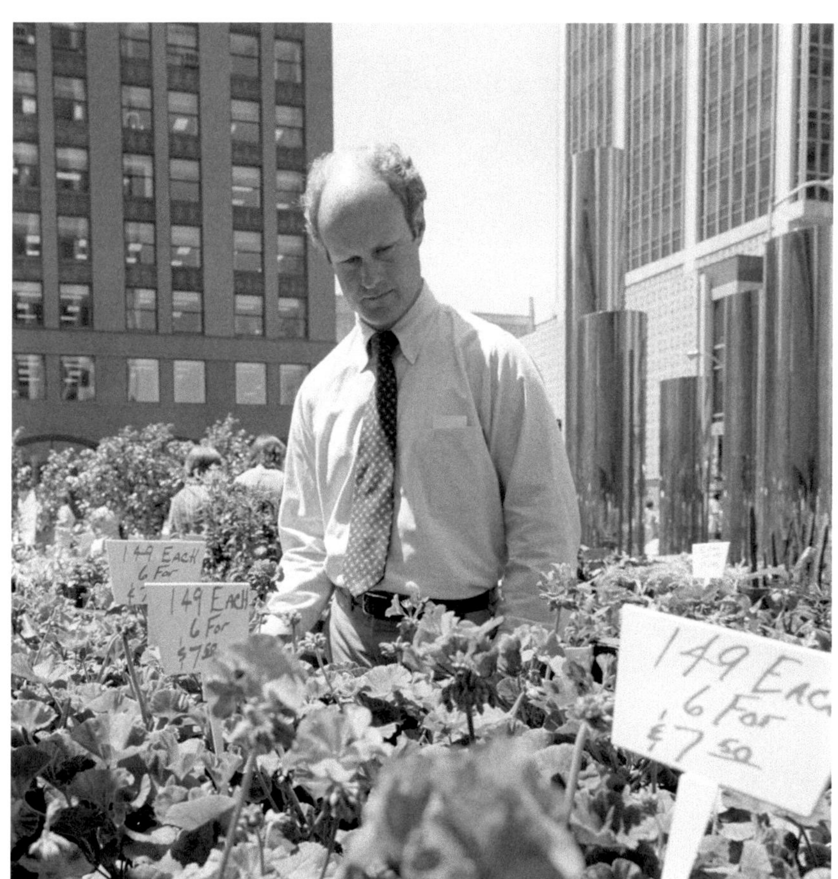
149 EACH
6 For
$7 50

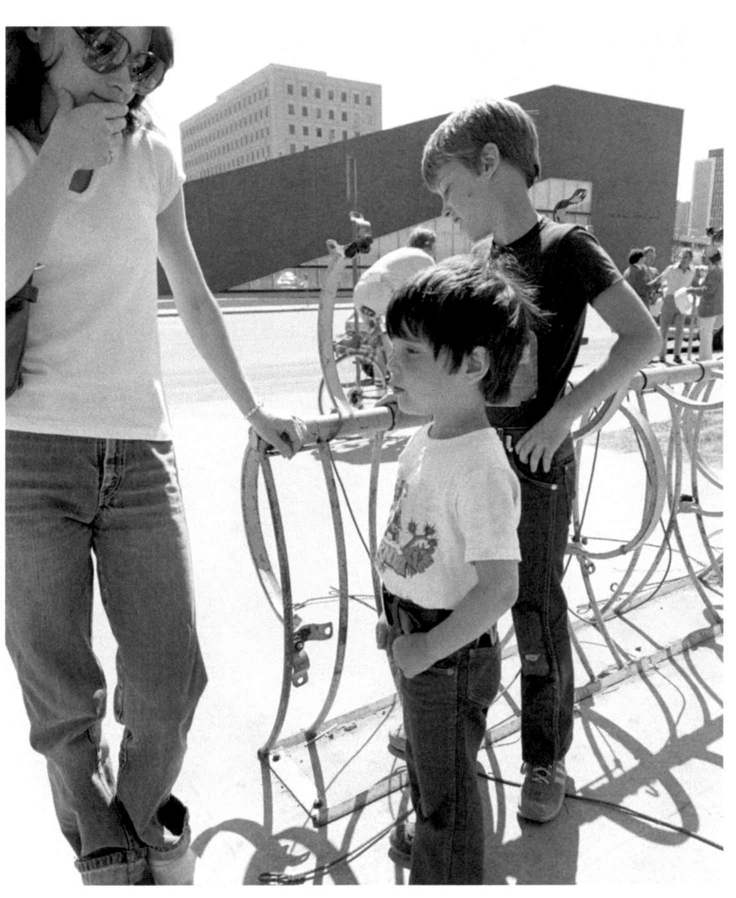

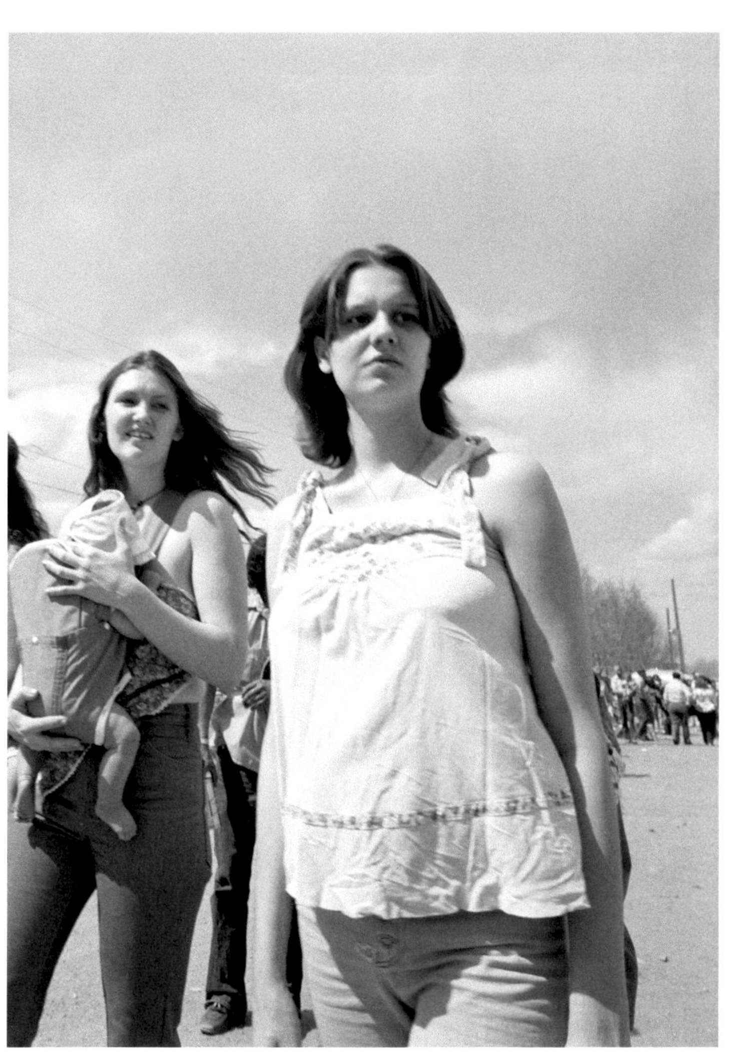

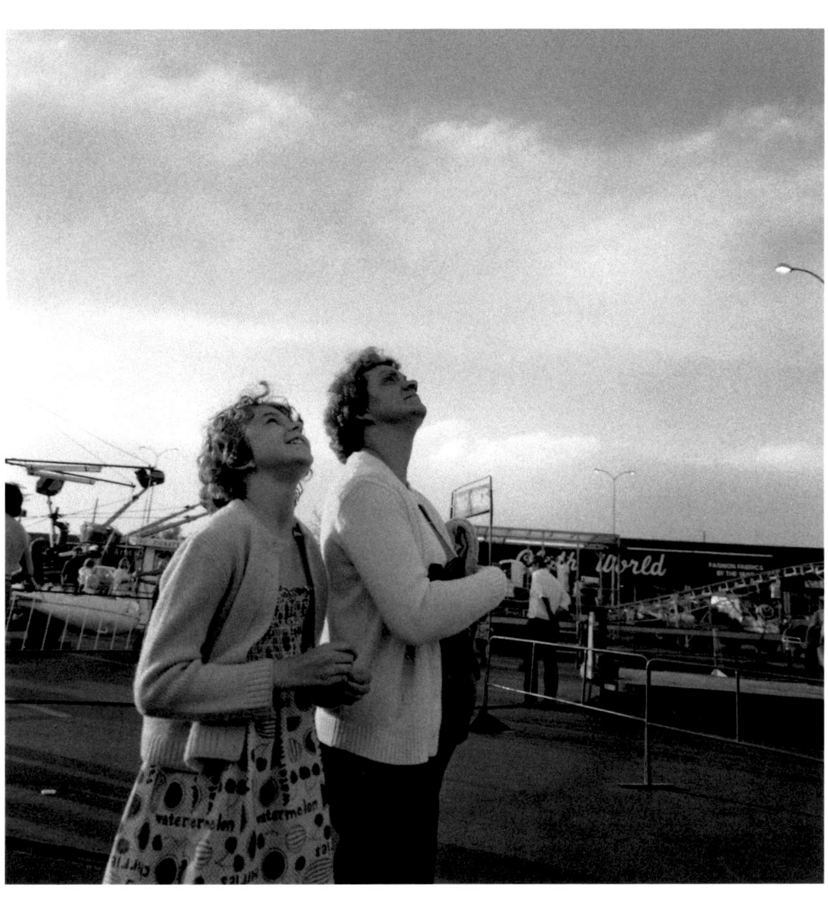
World
watermelon

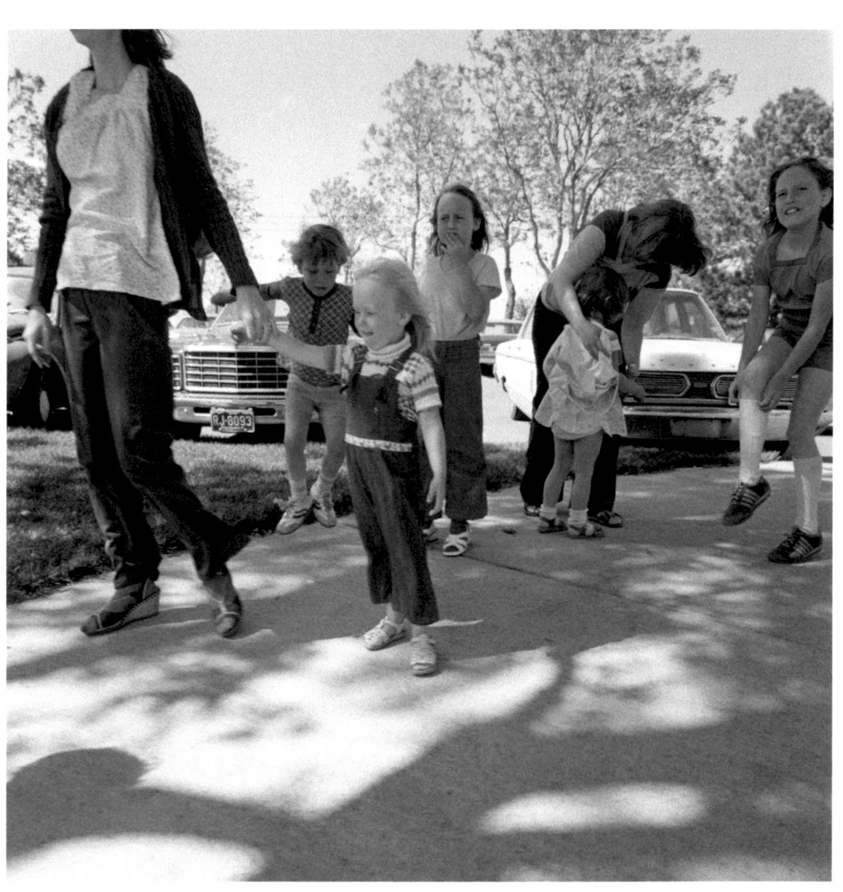
RJ-8093

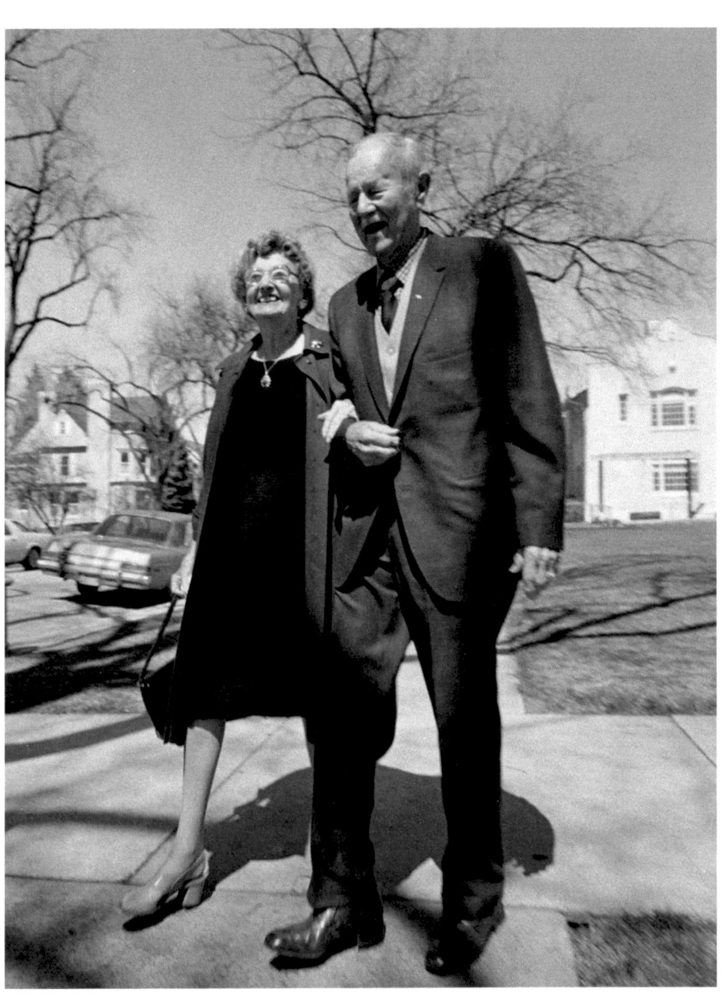

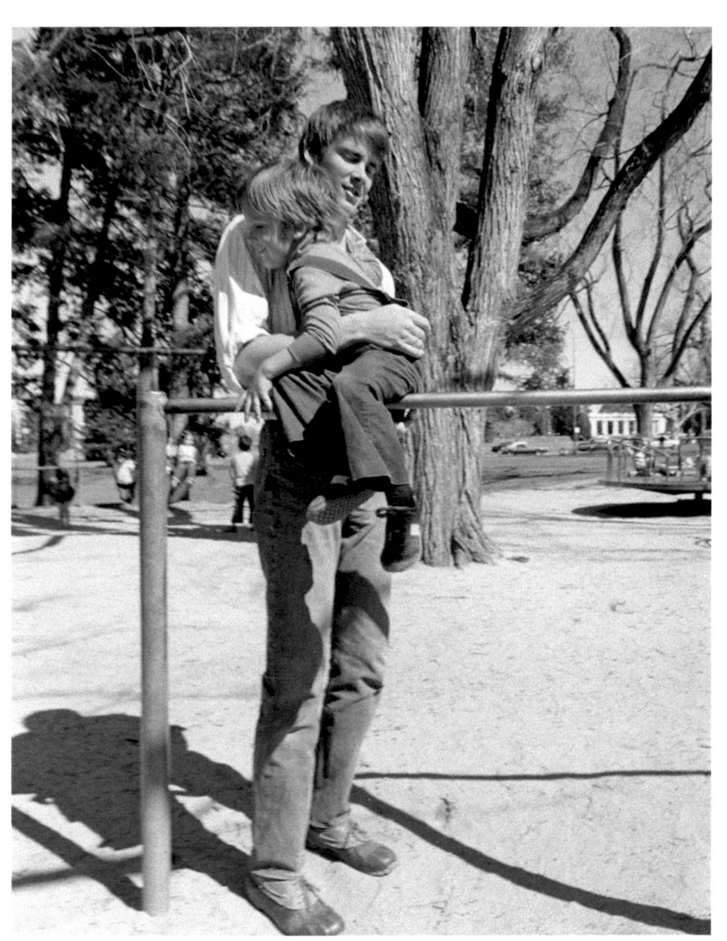

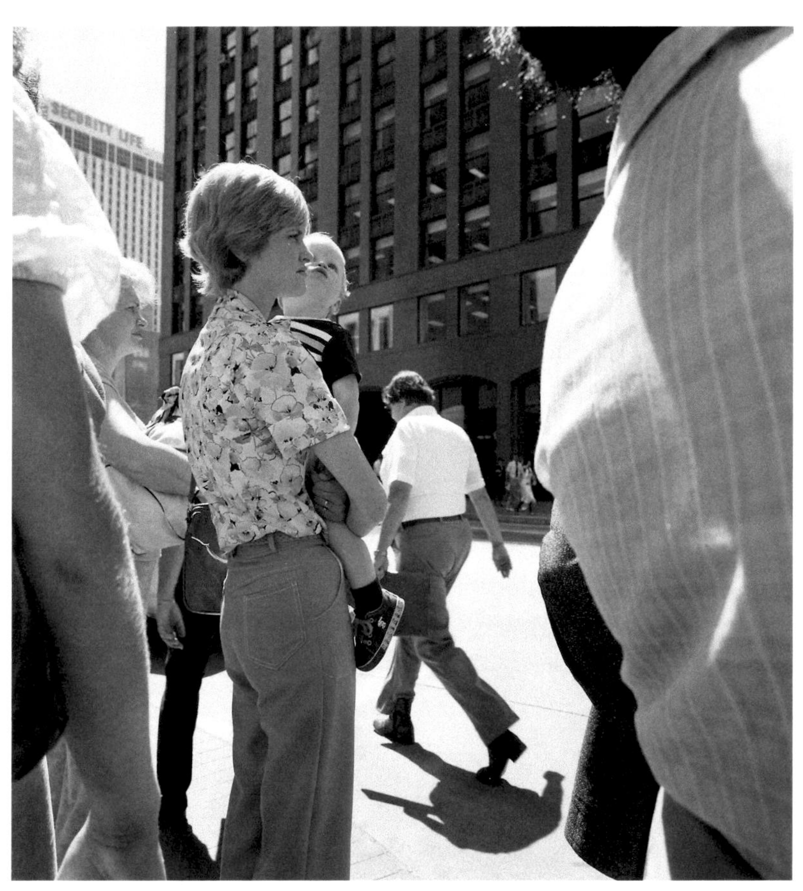
SECURITY LIFE

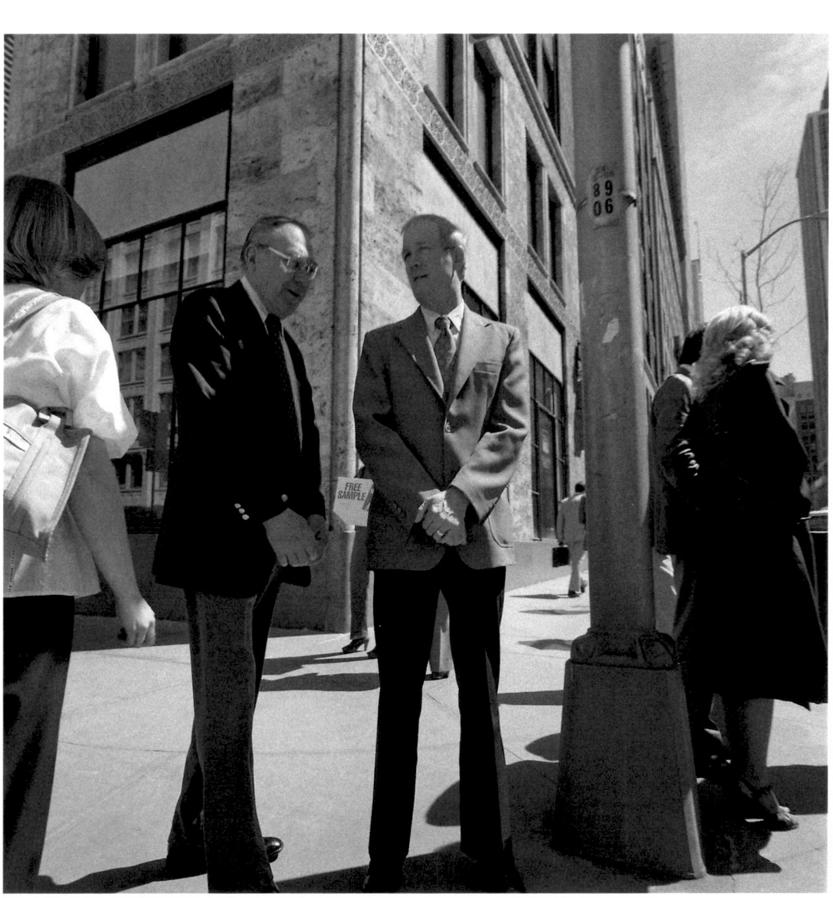
89
06
FREE
SAMPLE

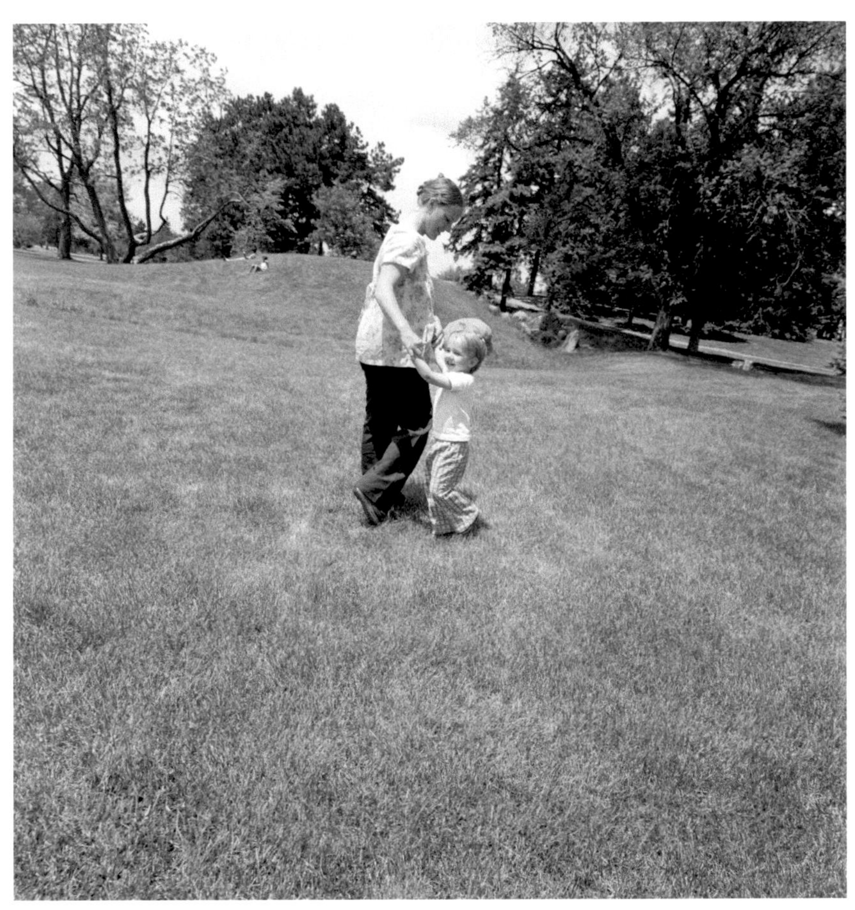

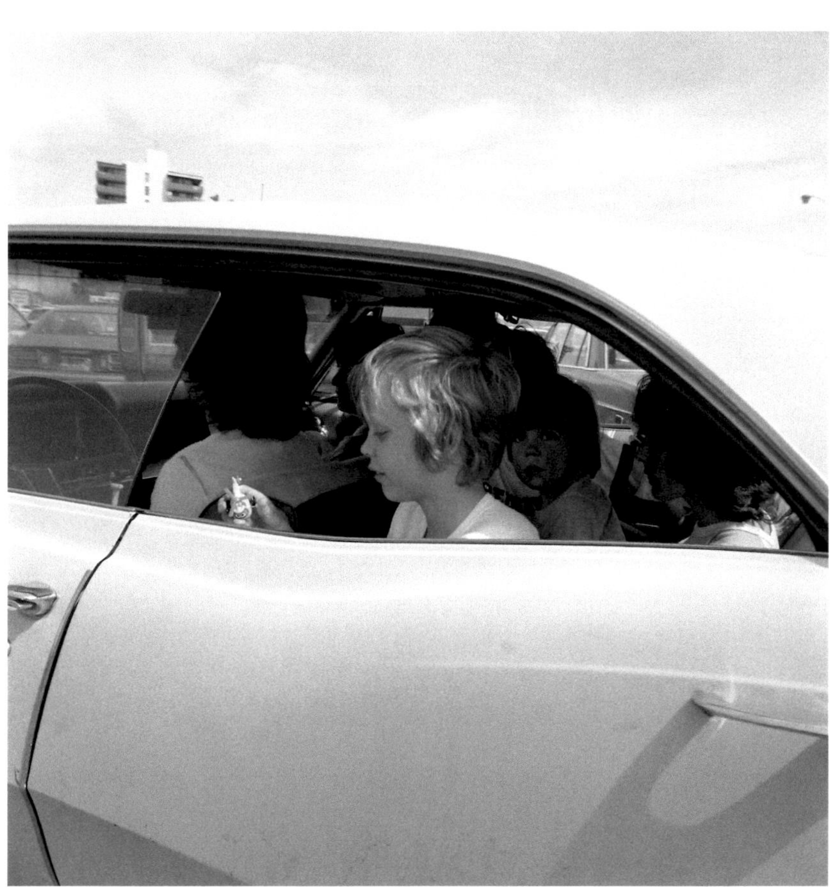

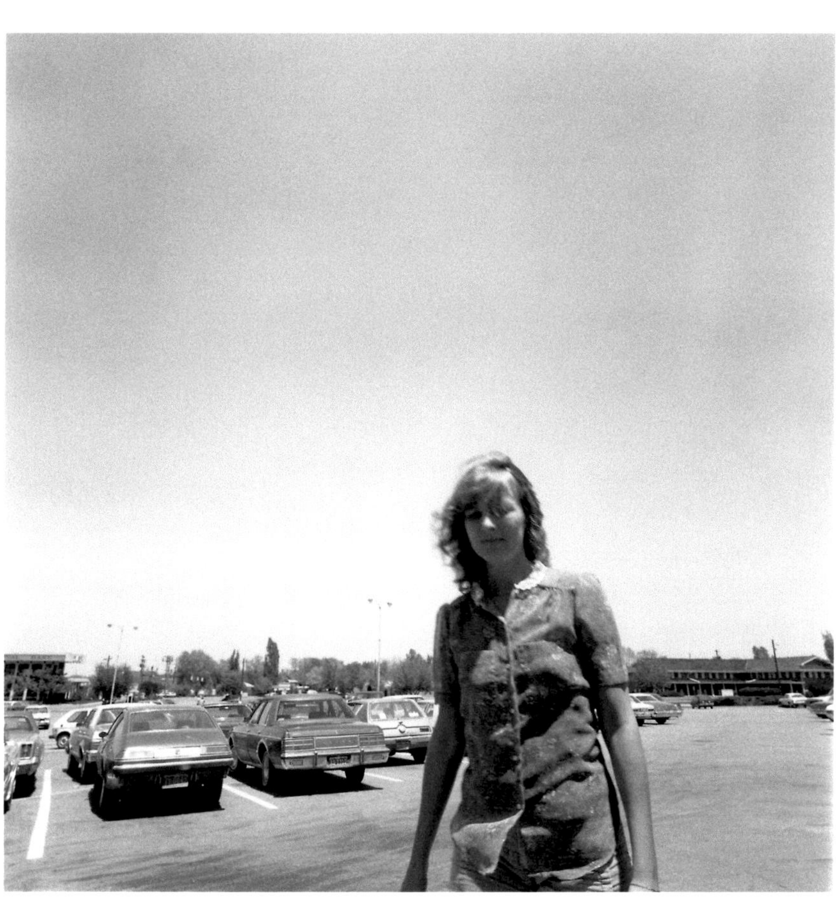

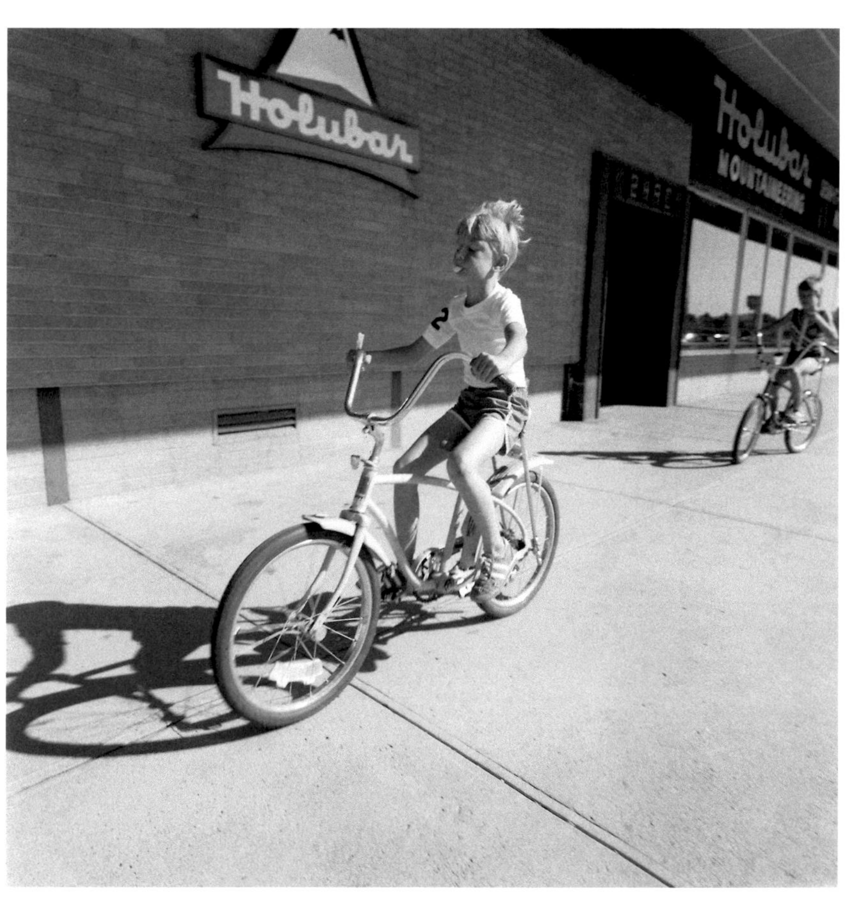
Holubar
Holubar
MOUNTAINEERING

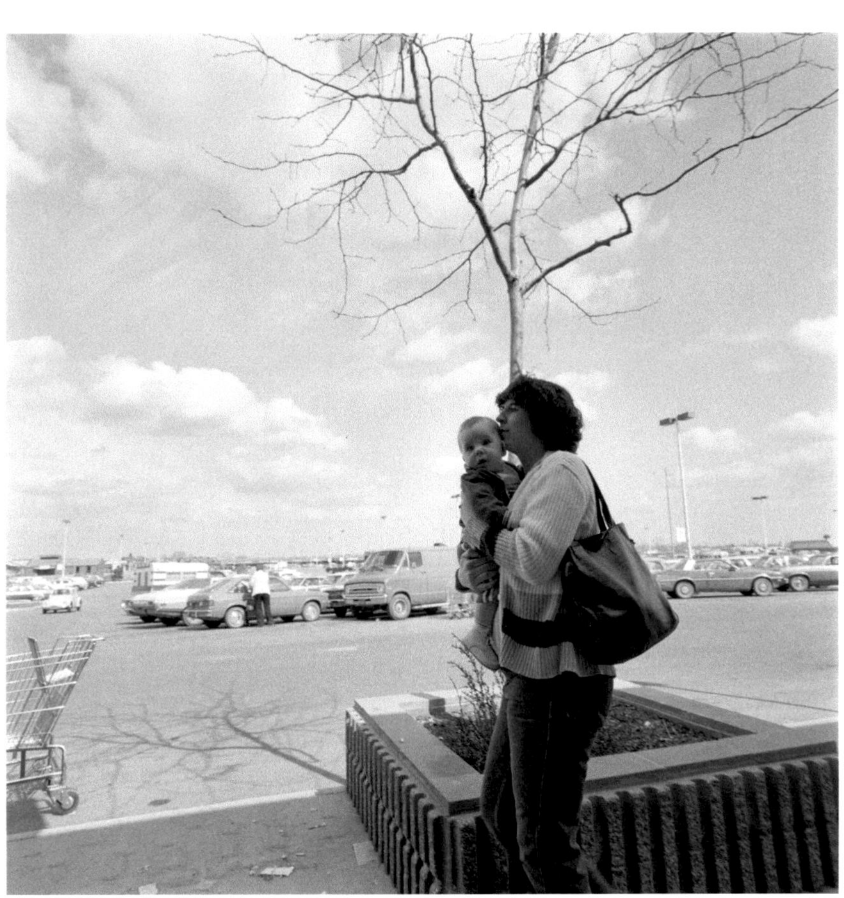

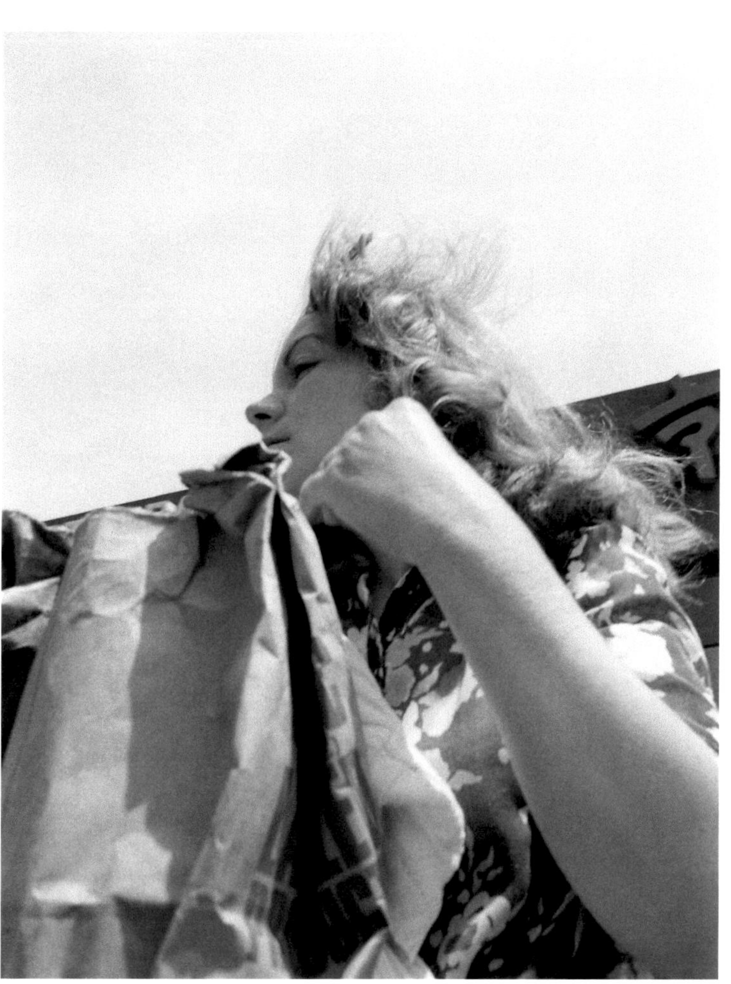

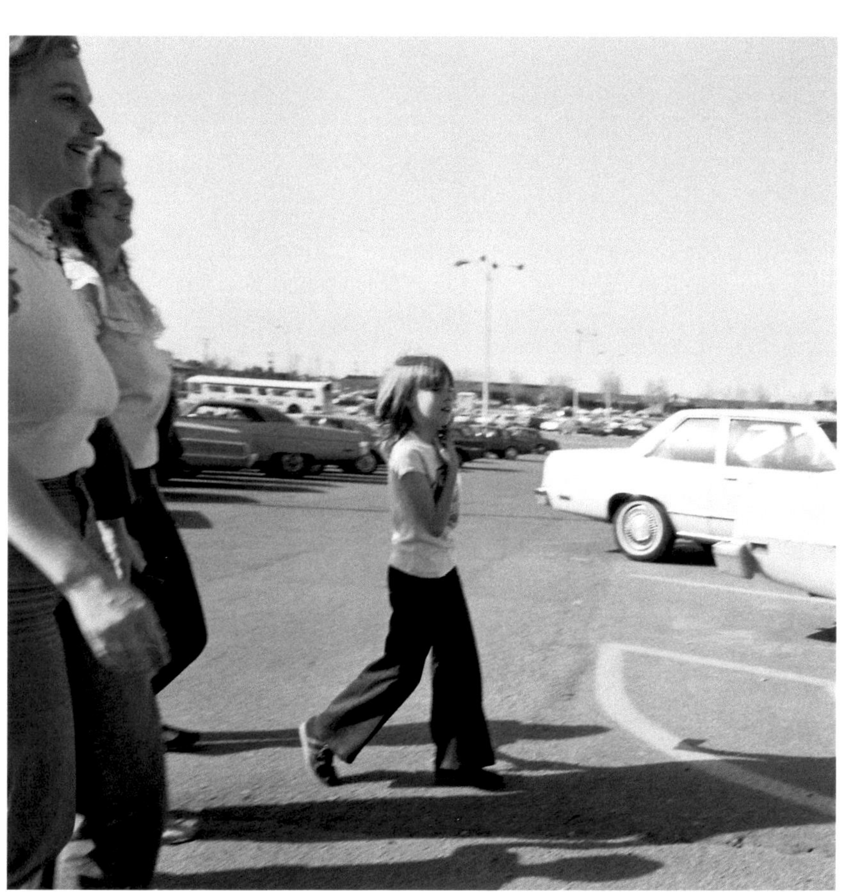

La question de l’espoir est aujourd’hui d’une urgence dramatique. Parmi les dangers qui menacent nos avenirs collectifs et individuels, figurent le terrorisme et l’exploitation abusive du monde naturel que nous partageons. Le point commun de bon nombre de ces crises, c’est qu’en tant qu’espèce vivante nous nous les infligeons à nous-mêmes.

Ces photographies ont été prises par Robert Adams entre 1979 et 1982 aux environs d’une usine d’armes nucléaires du Colorado. Les protestations des citoyens ont abouti à la fermeture de cette usine en 1989, mais les dommages causés à l’environnement et à la santé publique demeurent.

Alors que nous réfléchissons une fois encore aux conséquences d’une éventuelle catastrophe nucléaire, ce qui aujourd’hui ressort surtout de ces images ce sont les gestes – aussi discrets et fugaces soient-ils – d’affection, de tendresse et d’amour pour nos semblables.

Joshua Chuang

Misschien had geen tijd ooit zo'n grote nood aan hoop als de onze. Terrorisme en het systematische misbruik van de natuur verduisteren het uitzicht op toekomst voor mensen en gemeenschappen. En net als bij veel andere recente bedreigingen heeft de mensheid dit aan zichzelf te danken.

Robert Adams maakte al deze foto's in de jaren 1979–1982 in de buurt van een kernwapenfabriek in de Amerikaanse staat Colorado. In 1989 werd de fabriek na aanhoudend burgerprotest gesloten. Nu, dertig jaar later, dragen het milieu en de volksgezondheid nog steeds de gevolgen van de vroegere exploitatie.

Nu we opnieuw afwegen welke schade een kernramp zou kunnen aanrichten, is het meest opvallende aan deze foto's misschien wel de zorg en tederheid die mensen elkaar kunnen betonen – vluchtige tekens tegen de wanhoop die aangeven dat we niet geheel machteloos zijn.

Joshua Chuang

This publication is issued on the occasion of the exhibition *Robert Adams: A Right to Stand* at Fondation A Stichting, Brussels, from January to March 2018 with the cooperation of Fraenkel Gallery in San Francisco and Matthew Marks Gallery in New York.

The title is a quotation by the French writer Georges Bernanos: « L'espérance est un risque à courir ».

Fondation A Stichting
Astrid Ullens de Schooten Whettnall (President),
Jean-Paul Deridder (Director), Marta Bassan (Assistant)

Special thanks to Robert and Kerstin Adams, Jeffrey Fraenkel, Frish Brandt, Ola Dlugosz, Jeffrey Peabody, Cynthia Garvey

Design and publication coordination Hartmann Projects

Published by
Hartmann Books, Rulfinger Strasse 18, 70567 Stuttgart, Germany
www.hartmannprojects.com

Editing Joann Skrypzak-Davidsmeyer
Translation Brice Matthieussent (French), Wouter Meeus (Dutch)
Color separation Jan Scheffler, Prints Professional
Printing and binding DZA Druckerei zu Altenburg GmbH

ISBN 978-3-96070-016-6

Fondation A Stichting
Av. Van Volxelm, 304 bte1
B – 1190 Brussels
www.fondationastichting.be